TERESA CELSI

GOLF

The Lore of the Links

GOLF: THE LORE OF THE LINKS

copyright © 1992 by Armand Eisen.

All rights reserved. Printed in Hong Kong.

No part of this book may be used or reproduced in any manner whatsoever without written permission except in the case of reprints in the context of reviews.

For information write Andrews and McMeel, a Universal Press Syndicate Company, 4900 Main Street, Kansas City, Missouri 64112

10 9 8 7

ISBN: 0-8362-3019-1

Library of Congress Catalog Card Number: 91-77090

TABLE OF CONTENTS

INTRODUCTION

Golf is one of the most fascinating sports in the world. The object of it seems simple, childish even: take a stick and hit a small ball into a small hole. Nothing very difficult about that. But, like all good games, it takes minutes to learn and a lifetime to master.

Golf is a solitary and lonely game. No matter that a player is accompanied by caddies, two opponents and a partner, and possibly a crowd of admiring spectators—eventually the whole game comes down to one person, one club, and one ball, alone against the vagaries of nature. Anything can spoil a shot: a hazard, a puff of wind, a blade of grass. It seems too degrading to say that luck plays a factor in the game; some shots seem to be determined by a higher agency, not luck but inexorable fate itself.

In these pages you'll find the history of this royal and ancient game, the collected wit and wisdom of golf's immortals, stories of amazing feats and flubs on the links, and more. This little volume may not straighten out your tee shots or help prevent three-putting, but it just may help ease "the rub of the green."

PART I

A ROYAL AND ANCIENT GAME
The History
of Golf

ANCIENT ROOTS

The origins of golf are shrouded in the mysteries of time. One theory is that golf began in Rome as the pastime of bored shepherds. The top of a shepherd's crook curves (not unlike a golf club) and some have deduced that the shepherds started batting rocks or nuts around on the ground with the tool. Surrounded by sheep, nature's lawn mowers, they would have had an ideal surface to play on, and possibly natural holes made by rabbits or some other animal.

This rustic pastime might have been the roots of a game called *paganica*, which was played by the Roman Legions in the first century B.C. The game involved hitting a leather ball approximately five to seven inches in diameter around the countryside with a bent stick. Although the basic techniques of this game are known, its object is not. It's possible that the Legions played *paganica* while occupying parts of Britain and Scotland. The theory is that when the Roman Legions withdrew, the game remained, played by the native Scots and later refined into golf.

THE DUTCH CONNECTION

Another theory has golf beginning in Holland. The Dutch played a game with clubs that had brass and wooden heads. The object was to hit a small ball toward a post, located at either end of an enclosed area. This game was sometimes played on ice (when it was called *kolven*), sometimes on ground (when it was known as *kolf*), but always in an enclosed area. Excavations in Holland have yielded a small wooden ball and several ancient clubs. Kolf was perhaps closer to hockey and croquet than golf, but there is still a strong case to be made for Dutch influence on the game. The Dutch word for hole is *put.* A Dutch phrase used in kolf, *Stuit mij* ("It stops me"), is pronounced "Sty me." Later, the Dutch would be manufacturers of excellent golf balls, which were in great demand even in Scotland.

MEDIEVAL COUSINS

A game similar to kolf, but played in the open countryside, and not in an enclosure, developed in France and Belgium. Called *chole*, or *choula*, it involved two teams of two players and two balls. A target was set up, about a mile from the beginning point of the game. The target might be the steps of the local church, a gate, or the door of the local tavern. Each side was allowed three strokes on its ball, then the opposing team would play the ball for three strokes. The object was to make as much distance as possible on your three strokes, and then to pitch your opponents' ball into a hazard or similar difficulty. The first team to hit the target won.

A game played in Britain, *cambuca*, involved hitting a small ball made of box-root. It was banned, along with other games, in 1363. But a stained-glass panel showing a cambuca player still exists in the east window of Gloucester Cathedral. It depicts a man, clad in a medieval robe, in mid-backswing and showing pretty good golf form. (Although a friend might advise him to try keeping his left arm a bit straighter!)

OUT OF THE MOORS

But however much these early games contributed to golf, the game as it is known today is generally acknowledged to have developed in Scotland. The first written record of golf appeared in 1457, during the reign of James II. Scotland was at war at the time, and its parliament issued an act declaring that "the futeball and golfe be utterly cryed downe and not be used." The purpose of this was to prevent young men from wasting time better spent (according to the Parliament) practicing archery. The Scots put little faith in the military effectiveness of beaning an opponent on the head with a golf ball.

In 1503, James IV of Scotland married one of the daughters of Henry VII, and so brought golf to England. By the next generation, Henry VIII's first wife, Catherine of Aragon, would write a letter in which she describes her preoccupation "with the Golfe." (It is interesting to note that Henry VIII was thus one of the first golf widows—or golf widowers, as the case may be. His behavior toward his spouse has been emulated, more or less, by golf widows ever since.)

Other early references to golf show its continuing popularity with royalty. In 1567, Mary Queen of Scots was reported to have been seen playing on the links at St. Andrews shortly after the murder of her husband, Lord Darnley. In 1646, Charles I received the news of the Rebellion while playing at Leith. In 1682, James II of Scotland played the first international match with a couple of Englishmen at Holyrood. His partner was a local shoe-maker (and obviously a good shotmaker as well) named John Paterson. When they won, the prince awarded the stakes of the match to Paterson, who used the money to build a house.

THE FIRST COUNTRY CLUBS

The first golf club was the Honorable Company of Edinburgh Golfers, formed in 1744 in Leith. It disbanded in 1831 and moved to Musselburgh, where it resumed in 1836. Ten years after the formation of the Honorable Company, the St. Andrews Society of Golfers was organized. Each member contributed five shillings toward a silver cup to be awarded each year in competition. The St. Andrews Society (which later changed its name to the Royal and Ancient Golf Club of St. Andrews) still survives and is the oldest golf club continuously in existence.

St. Andrews set the standards for modern golf. Originally, the course consisted of twenty-two holes. In 1764, some of the holes were combined in order to make the course more difficult. This lowered the number of holes to eighteen. From then on, the standard number of holes per round has been eighteen. The basic rules for the first competition, written in 1754, still stand with very few changes.

The first record of golf in North America dates from 1657. A court record of Fort Orange in New Netherland (Albany, New York) mentions fines levied for playing golf in the streets. There are several references to a golf club in 1786, at Charleston Green in Charleston, South

Carolina. Another club was organized in Savannah, Georgia before 1800. Both clubs apparently existed until the War of 1812. They may have disbanded due to the general anti-British sentiment following the war. It took a long time for golf to return to the New World. The Royal Montreal Golf Club, officially recognized as the first golf club in North America, was not formed until 1873.

In 1888, the first modern golf course in the United States was laid out in Yonkers, New York. It consisted of three holes in a cow pasture. A club was formed, called St.

Andrews in honor of the Royal and Ancient Club in Scotland. It was an inauspicious beginning, but foretold a coming golf explosion.

THE RISE OF THE USGA

In 1895, there were seventy-five different clubs in the country. By 1900 there were over 1,000. The Amateur Golf Association of the United States, which later became the United States Golf Association (USGA), was created in 1894 to establish uniform rules and to conduct championships. In 1895, the Association held its first tournament, consisting of an Amateur Championship, a professional Open, and a Women's Amateur Championship.

Part of the function of the USGA was to establish the rules of golf in the United States. The ultimate authority worldwide was St. Andrews in Scotland. The USGA simply adopted the St. Andrews rules, but occasionally the two authorities differed. One of the more interesting divergences was in the matter of golf balls. In 1931, the USGA set the maximum diameter of golf balls at 1.68 inches. St. Andrews determined the standard to be a maximum of 1.62 inches. This meant that for years, golfers would play one type of ball in the United States and a different one in Great Britain. In 1990, St. Andrews finally adopted the USGA standard, and that is now the standard for the world.

SPANNING THE GLOBE . . .
AND BEYOND

The spread of golf worldwide can be attributed to the spread of the British Empire. As British residents colonized the world, they brought their clubs with them and hacked their courses out of the wilderness. The first golf club in Australia dates from 1870, the first club in New Zealand from 1873. The first two clubs in South Africa were formed in 1884 and 1885. The British were playing golf in Calcutta in 1829 and in Bombay in 1842.

British railroad engineers brought the game to South America. In 1890, clubs were formed in Brazil and Uruguay. The first Argentinian club started in 1908. The highest golf course in the world is located in Bolivia, 12,149 feet above sea level.

But the biggest explosion in golf came in the Orient, and mainly since the Second World War. In 1903, a nine-hole course was built by British residents on Mount Rokko in Japan. Another course was soon laid out inside a Yokohama racetrack, and in 1914, the first course built by the Japanese was the Tokyo Golf Club. In 1924, the Japan Golf Association was formed, adopting the Royal and Ancient rules. In 1930, pros Joe Kirkwood and

Walter Hagen toured Japan. Because of the interest spurred by this tour and the next one by Bill Melhorn and Bobby Cruikshank, thirty new courses were built and golf became a part of the Japanese business establishment.

Japanese golf was interrupted by World

War II, but by 1950, it was going strong again, this time under USGA rules. In 1957, the World Cup matches were held in Tokyo. Twenty-nine visiting teams from all around the world played, but the winners were favorite sons Torakichi Nakamura and Koichi Ono. The victory spurred a national craze. It is estimated that there are more than three million golf players in Japan today, and most of them will never get the chance to actually play on a golf course. The land in Japan is too precious and scarce to build enough courses to fill the demand. Instead, most Japanese play only on driving ranges, some of which are three stories high.

PART II

WHAT A SHOT!
Strange But True
Tales From the
Course

Up, Up, and Away

Once, at the twelfth hole of the Augusta National, Bob Rosburg was hitting into the wind. To compensate, he hit with tremendous drive. Just as he swung, the wind died. Up, up, up in the air the ball sailed, clear on past the putting green, past all the hazards, clear out of bounds. It finally landed on the ninth hole—of a different country club. Rosburg took the penalty, re-teed, and still managed to finish the hole with five.

Ace Cadet

Some players are just born great. Witness Ben Crenshaw. At the age of 9, he took his first lesson with Harvey Penick, one of the greatest golf teachers in the country. Mr. Penick began by having Ben hit a ball. On the first swing, the ball landed on the green.

Penick was too experienced a teacher to be impressed by a lucky first shot. He began walking toward the green. "Now let's see you knock it into the hole," he said.

"Why didn't you tell me that in the first place?" Ben asked. And with that, he set down another ball, swung, and, on his second-ever swing, made his first ace.

Thanks, Honey

Ben Hogan's wife, Valerie, accompanied him on his tours. One night, she was watching him practice putting in their hotel room. After sitting patiently for some time, she offered him a bit of advice.

"All you have to do is hit the ball closer to the hole," she said.

Like Father, Like Son

Golfer Tommy Bolt is known for his sweet swing and foul temper. While giving a clinic to a group of amateurs, Bolt tried to show his softer side by involving his fourteen-year-old son in the lesson.

"Show the nice folks what I taught you," said Bolt. His son obediently took a nine-iron, cursed, and hurled it into the sky.

Saint Bobby

Good sportsmanship is the essence of golf, and no one exemplified that more than Bobby Jones. In the 1925 U.S. Open, Jones's ball moved when he addressed it. No one else had seen it move, so Jones called the penalty on himself. That penalty ended up costing him the championship.

"There's only one way to play the game," he said when later asked about it. "You might as well praise a man for not robbing a bank as to praise him for playing by the rules."

Next Time,
Just Ask for an Autograph

Golf takes a tremendous amount of concentration. When that concentration is shattered, the effects can be devastating. In 1940, Lawson Little was in a playoff with Gene Sarazen when a fan approached him with a question about whether he inhaled or exhaled on his backswing.

The next three swings were ruined as Little tried in vain to figure it out.

Presidential Tales

Ulysses S. Grant was the first president to visit a golf course. He went with a friend, who was trying to entice the president to take up the sport. After watching for a few moments, Grant turned to his friend and remarked: "That does look like very good exercise. But what's the little white ball for?"

President Dwight D. Eisenhower was an avid golfer with a so-so game. Shortly after leaving office, he was asked if leaving the White House had affected his play. He responded, "It must have. A lot more people beat me now."

Bad Bounce

Gary Player hooked his shot on the last hole at Huddersfield. The ball came to rest near a stone wall. Told he needed four to win the match, he decided he couldn't afford the penalty of an unplayable lie. His only chance was to try and ricochet the ball off the wall. He smashed the ball. It hit the wall and flew right back at him, hitting him on the chin.

Player was knocked out cold, but, recovering, he went on to make the hole in four. Unfortunately, hitting himself with the ball gave him a two-stroke penalty, giving him six for the hole. He ended up losing the tournament by a stroke.

Maybe for You, Mr. Jones

Acomplaint was made to golf immortal and course architect Robert Trent Jones that a hole he designed was too difficult to play. Wishing to accommodate those players who complained, Jones joined them in a foursome on the course, just to test the hole.

He was the last to tee up, and watched as each of the others hit their balls squarely onto the green. Then Jones swung. His ball sailed down the fairway, onto the green, and into the hole for an ace. For a moment there was a profound silence.

"Gentlemen, I think this hole is eminently fair," Jones said at last.

In the Can

A Scottish amateur, Freddie Tait, found after a shot that his ball had landed inside a condensed-milk can. Instead of taking an unplayable lie, he swung at the can. It landed on the green, and the ball rolled out and stopped right next to the hole.

The Martyrdom of St. Jacklin

Life isn't fair, and neither is golf. Tony Jacklin was playing Lee Trevino at Muirfield in 1972. Trevino managed to sink two outrageous putts in a row, getting birdies on both the fourteenth and fifteenth holes. On the next hole, Trevino's shot went high. By all rights it should have flown over the green. Instead, it hit the flagstick three feet in the air and dropped straight down into the hole. Jacklin had been playing well all round, but this was Trevino's third birdie in as many holes. On the seventeenth hole,

Trevino again sunk a long putt for a birdie.

Things were looking up for Jacklin on the eighteenth hole. Trevino overshot the green. His swing on the recovering chip shot was far too strong. But Jacklin's heart, which had leapt with the arc of the ball, sank just as fast when the ball again caught the flagstick and dropped straight down into the hole. Trevino immediately declared his luck proof that God must be a Mexican. He went on to win the Open. As for Jacklin, it's been said that his game has never been the same since.

Aye, Chingy

The caddie, of course, is more than just a nameless face who carries the clubs. His advice can be invaluable—when the players take it. At Sunningdale, Neil Coles and his caddie Arthur "Chingy" Maidmont got into an argument over which club to use on a particular shot. Soon they were playing tug o' war, as Coles strove to wrest his four-iron from the protesting Chingy. Finally Coles won. He stepped up to the ball, swung, and landed his ball on the green, four feet from the flag. He glared back at his caddie in triumph.

"You would have been closer with the three-iron," Chingy said.

Le Twilight Zone

Philippe Porquier was playing in his first tournament. At one hole, after two shots, he was a scant forty yards from the pin. He shanked his next shot at a ninety-degree angle to the pin and out of bounds. Porquier dropped another ball, and promptly shanked it. Again and again he shanked his simple chip.

Finally, Porquier aimed at a point ninety degrees to the *left* of the green. He swung. The ball shanked right onto the green. He sank the ball in two putts and entered history with twenty-one strokes—the most ever recorded for one hole in the European Tour.

The Soul of Tact

When Bobby Jones first started out, he played the National Open Championship paired with the legendary Harry Vardon. The young Jones was too awed by the great player (who had been his hero since he was a boy) to say anything. So they played the first round in silence.

One the second round, at the seventh hole, Jones's first shot was good. It landed just a little short of the green, and it seemed inevitable that he would make par and would probably birdie the hole. But when Jones pitched the ball, he topped it, and it leapt over the green and into a bunker. Instead of his expected birdie, he ended up bogeying.

As he walked to the next tee, embarrassed by one of the worst shots in his life, he finally broke the ice with Vardon.

"Mr. Vardon, did you ever see a worse shot than that?" he asked.

"No," Vardon replied. Jones declares this the most conclusive estimate on a shot he's ever heard.

Water Hazard

One of the championships at St. Andrews was interrupted by a sudden storm. Maitland Dougall was just about to tee off on a seaside hole when the clouds burst. Out on the waves, a ship began to founder. Dougall sprang into a lifeboat and spent the next five hours helping to rescue the crew. Then he went back to the tee, continued the game, and won the title.

Stonewalled

In 1960, Arnold Palmer was playing at St. Andrews, where the seventeenth hole is acknowledged as one of the most difficult in golf. Each of the first three rounds of competition, Palmer had three-putted the hole. In the final round, he realized that he had to improve that average to win the competition.

The first three times he played the hole, he had used a six-iron for his approach. This time, in defiance of common sense, Palmer pulled out his five-iron. The ball overshot the green, hit a stone wall behind it, and bounced back to the pin. For the first time, Palmer made par on the hole.

Killer Butterflies

In 1922, Gene Sarazen and Ben Hogan played a special Challenge Match, just between the two of them. Sarazen won the match, but complained that it had been the most grueling golf of his life. His stomach had been in knots the whole time. He attributed this to nerves—until he saw a doctor. The doctor admitted Sarazen to the hospital for emergency surgery. They managed to remove his appendix just before it burst.

THE
QUOTABLE
GOLFER

Golf is a game whose aim is to hit a very small ball into a very small hole, with weapons singularly ill-designed for the purpose.

—WINSTON CHURCHILL

The average golfer doesn't play golf. He attacks it.

—JACKIE BURKE

Golf appeals to the idiot in us and the child. What child does not grasp the simple pleasure-principle of miniature golf? Just how childlike golf players become is proven by their frequent inability to count past five.

—JOHN UPDIKE

Golf is the hardest game in the world. There's no way you can ever get it. Just when you think you do, the game jumps up and puts you into your place.

—BEN CRENSHAW

Golf is a game of expletives not deleted.

—Dr. Irving A. Gladstone

Golf is a game in which you yell fore, shoot six, and write down five.

—Paul Harvey

Golf combines two favorite American pastimes: taking long walks and hitting things with a stick.

—P. J. O'Rourke

Golf is a good walk spoiled.

—Mark Twain

You have to make corrections in your game a little bit at a time. It's like taking your medicine. A few aspirin will probably cure what ails you, but the whole bottle might just kill you.

—HARVEY PENICK

The player may experiment about his swing, his grip, his stance. It is only when he begins asking his caddie's advice that he is getting on dangerous ground.

—SIR WALTER SIMPSON

There are two things the players on tours should realize: Adults will copy your swing, and young people will follow your example.

—HARVEY PENICK

Caddies are a breed of their own. If you shoot sixty-six, they say, "Man, we shot sixty-six!" But go out and shoot seventy-seven, and they say, "Hell, he shot seventy-seven!"

—LEE TREVINO

I love to sweat and heave and breathe and hurt and burn and get dirty…. There's something good about getting all dirty and grimy and nasty and then showering; you feel twice as clean.

—JAN STEPHENSON

I may be the only golfer never to have broken a single putter, if you don't count the one I twisted into a loop and threw into a bush.

—THOMAS BOSWELL

If you pick up a golfer and hold it close to your ear, like a conch shell, and listen, you will hear an alibi.

—FRED BECK

Mulligan: invented by an Irishman who wanted to hit one more twenty-yard grounder.

—JIM BISHOP

Give me golf clubs, the fresh air, and a beautiful partner, and you can keep my golf clubs and the fresh air.

—JACK BENNY

I say this without any reservations whatsoever: It is impossible to outplay an opponent you can't outthink.

—LAWSON LITTLE

Give me a man with big hands, big feet, and no brains and I will make a golfer out of him.

—WALTER HAGEN

The most exquisitely satisfying act in the world of golf is that of throwing a club. The full backswing, the delayed wrist action, the flowing follow-through, followed by that unique whirring sound, reminiscent only of a passing flock of starlings, are without parallel in sport.

—HENRY LONGHURST

When you reflect on the combination of characteristics that golf demands of those who would presume to play it, it is not surprising that golf has never had a truly great player who was not also a person of extraordinary character.

—FRANK D. "SANDY" TUTAM, JR.

The hardest shot is a mashie at ninety yards from the green, where the ball has to be played against an oak tree, bounced back into a sand trap, hits a stone, bounces on the green, and then rolls into the cup. That shot is so difficult I have only made it once.

—ZEPPO MARX

I never pray on the golf course. Actually, the Lord answers my prayers everywhere except on the course.

—REV. BILLY GRAHAM

Let's face it, 95 percent of this game is mental. A guy plays lousy golf, he doesn't need a pro, he needs a shrink.

—TOM MURPHY

Charley hits some good woods—most of them are trees.

—GLEN CAMPBELL,
on his friend Charley Pride

Anyone who criticizes a golf course is like a person invited to a house for dinner who, on leaving, tells the host that the food was lousy.

—GARY PLAYER

▼

A golf course is the epitome of all that is purely transitory in the universe, a space not to dwell in, but to get over as quickly as possible.

—JEAN GIRAUDOUX

If your adversary is a hole or two down, there is no serious cause for alarm in his complaining of a severely sprained wrist.... Should he happen to win the next hole, these symptoms will in all probability become less troublesome.

—HORACE G. HUTCHINSON

It's good sportsmanship to not pick up lost golf balls while they're still rolling.

—MARK TWAIN

Baffling late-life discovery: Golfers wear those awful clothes on purpose.

—HERB CAEN

The golfer has more enemies than any other athlete. He has fourteen clubs in his bag, all of them different; eighteen holes to play, all of them different, every week; and all around him are sand, trees, grass, water, wind, and 143 other players. In addition, the game is 50 percent mental, so his biggest enemy is himself.

—DAN JENKINS

Like life, golf can be humbling. However, little good comes from brooding about mistakes we've made. The next shot, in golf or in life, is the big one.

—GRANTLAND RICE

PART IV

STICKS, BALLS, AND BAGS
The Evolution of Equipment

"FEATHERIES"

The first round objects hit with a stick were in all probability nuts or rocks, but the first known golf balls were made of feathers. Known as "featheries," these balls served from golf's earliest days till the Victorian era. Each featherie was composed of "as much feathers as will fill a hat" stuffed tightly (and with great effort!) into a small sphere fashioned from leather or horsehide, soaked in alum. As the leather dried, it hardened and shrank, while the feathers expanded. This gave the ball a tight, hard surface (at least until it got damp). Often the balls were made of horsehide, which led someone to observe that the golf ball should be called "Pegasus—half horse, half bird."

They certainly flew like birds. The light weight of the ball helped it to catch the wind. The record for a flight of a featherie was set in 1836 at 361 yards.

EARLY STICKS

The first golf clubs were undoubtedly made of wood. Most likely they were bent sticks, or shepherds' crooks. But as golf progressed as a game, clubs evolved and club-making became an art.

The first record of golf clubs dates back to the time of James IV. In 1603, William Mayne received a Royal Warrant as club- and spear-maker from the king. Although the records exist, there are no surviving examples of these royal sticks. The oldest surviving clubs date from 1741. They were found in a closet of a house in Hull, England, and may date back as far as the Stuarts. The set consisted of six woods and two irons, all shafted with ash wood. The heads of the woods were reinforced with lead.

THE ART OF THE CLUB

The height of the art of club-making came in the early 1800s, at the end of the feather ball period in golf. Two particular club-makers, Hugh Philip and Douglas McEwen, became known as the Chippendale and Hepplewhite of golf. The clubs they designed had thick grips and sharply tapering shafts. The heads were long and slender, less than half an inch thick, perfect for the subtle requirements of hitting the lightweight and delicate featheries.

Douglas McEwen began a club by planting hedgethorn horizontally on hillsides. When the trees grew, they bent toward the sun at a perfect angle to form the neck of a club. McEwen cut these short, spliced in shafts of ash wood, and so crafted his clubs.

BUDDHA'S CONTRIBUTION
TO THE SPORT

In the 1840s a momentous discovery was made. It all started with a statue of Buddha, sent from Singapore to a British professor, Dr. Paterson, by his missionary son. The statue was packed in gutta percha, a type of dried gum from the sapodilla tree. Gutta percha can be melted and formed like wax, but when cooled it hardens like plastic. In 1845, another of Dr. Paterson's sons, Rob, came upon the idea of making a golf ball from gutta percha. He tried it out on the links. The first balls shattered after a few strokes, but he persisted and soon came up with a ball that lasted.

People were astonished at the ball's durability and distance, particularly in the rain. The featheries became damp, soggy, and useless when wet, but the gutta percha performed just as well as ever. And since the gutta percha could soon be mass-produced, it brought the prices of golf balls down to something that nearly anyone could afford, thus increasing the popularity of the game.

EARLY BAGS

The arrival of the gutta percha ball necessitated a change in club design.

The slender heads were too delicate to stand up under repeated whacks on the harder ball. The heads of the clubs soon became shorter and thicker in design.

In this period the number of different clubs increased to meet the different conditions and situations a golfer might encounter. An entire set might consist of seven woods and six irons. Of this number, thirteen in all, a player might carry eight clubs in a round. To carry this many clubs, a simple bag was fashioned out of sailcloth. This was the forerunner of the golf bag.

A BALL WITH GUTS

The next major innovation in golf balls came in the late nineteenth century. In 1898, Coburn Haskell, an avid golfer, stopped at the Goodrich rubber plant to pick up Bert Work for a round of golf. While he waited for his friend to finish work, Haskell saw some elastic thread lying on a table. Haskell started winding the thread around some rubber into a ball, and by the time his friend Work arrived, he had made a ball with a lively bounce. Envisioning the sensation the ball would cause when he teed off, he suggested that Work cover the ball with gutta percha.

Work decided to try his friend's half-serious suggestion. He gave the idea to his engineering staff, and they worked out the first rubber-cored golf ball. The ball flew farther, with more bounce, and putted with more accuracy than any previous type of ball.

It had long been known that gutta perchas performed best after a bit of "roughing" up in play. By the time the rubber-cored ball was developed, there were many different patterns in use. One, the "Agrippa" pattern, consisted of hundreds of raised pimples (called brambles). Haskell and Work used the Agrippa pattern for their new rubber-cored ball.

In 1899, Goodrich formally introduced the ball to the golfing world. The new balls flew farther than the gutta perchas, but they tended to bounce more erratically than the old balls. Opinion was divided on the innovation. Then, in 1901, Walter J. Travis won the USGA Amateur Championship with a Haskell ball. That ended the debate and the rubber-cored golf ball became the standard from that day on.

WHITE BALLS...

In 1903, Spaulding, which had acquired a license to produce a rubber-cored ball, brought out its "Spaulding Wizard." Two years later, it introduced the first truly white golf ball. Previously golf balls were painted white. Spaulding's new ball got its color not from paint, but from the color of the material, balata, which had the added advantages of being softer than gutta percha and less likely to nick.

...WITH DIMPLES

In 1906 William Taylor was given a patent for a very simple concept: the dimple. It was Taylor's contribution to golf to invert the bramble, resulting in the dimpled ball in use to this very day. Soon the manufacture of golf balls had become a science. Tests were made of different patterns and depths of dimples, and by 1930 the optimum depth of a dimple was determined to be between 0.012″ and 0.0125″ on a 1.62-inch ball. This is the standard which has caught on, and all modern balls use it.

NEWER CLUBS, BETTER CLUBS

With the introduction of the rubber-cored ball, the clubs had to adapt again. The rubber-cored ball was still harder and heavier than the gutta percha. Again, the face of the clubs were deepened and inset with metal. Various experiments were made with different metals, but not until 1924—when the Union Hardware Company of Torrington, Connecticut came up with a seamless shaft of high-carbon steel—did steel replace hickory as the shaft of choice.

It was shortly after this that club manufacturers came up with the idea of selling matched sets of clubs. Formerly each club was bought individually and distinguished by a colorful name (mashie, niblick, etc). The concept of selling sets of matched clubs caught on, and a new system of numbering the clubs was devised. In 1938, there were so many clubs in use that the USGA set the maximum number of clubs in a round to fourteen.

Since the introduction of the steel shaft, other materials have been tried, but none has completely replaced steel. Fiberglass was touted in the 1950s, but it produced a heavy club. Aluminum was supposed to revolutionize golf. Since it was such a lightweight metal, an aluminum club could have a heavier head than a steel club, and theoretically drive the ball farther. But many players dislike the balance of the aluminum clubs, which hasn't lived up to its billing as the club of the future. The same may one day be said of today's graphite and titanium clubs, whose supremacy over steel clubs is certain in one area only—exorbitant prices (over $125 per club, in some cases).

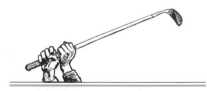

PRESERVING THE FUTURE

Today, the push is not to improve golf balls and equipment, but to make sure that technology does not outstrip skill and technique. Since 1942, the USGA has tested golf balls and clubs with a machine called "Iron Byron" (named after golf professional Byron Nelson). The maximum velocity allowed a golf ball is 250 feet per second. Any ball testing higher than that is declared unfair, unsafe, and downright illegal. In this way, it is hoped that the competitive spirit and simple soul of golf can be maintained, even as technology marches on.

GLOSSARY
OF
GOLF
TERMS

ALBATROSS: A score of three under par for a single hole. Also called a double eagle.

BANANA BALL: A bad slice, so called because the flight of the ball resembles the shape of a banana.

BARBER: A player who talks to the point of annoyance.

BISQUE: A handicap stroke given to one opponent that may be used on any hole.

COLLAR: Edge of a sand hazard.

CROSS-BUNKER: A narrow bunker that crosses a hole at a right angle to the player's line of flight to the green.

DORMIE: A situation in match play when a player or a side is ahead by the amount of holes remaining to be played. In such a case, the trailing player or side must win the remaining holes to come out even.

EAGLE: A score of two under par for a single hole.

FOOZLE: A bad shot. Also called a dub.

FRIED EGG: A ball that is buried in sand. Also called a plugged lie.

FROG HAIR: The short grass that borders the putting green.

GIMMEE: Baby talk for "give me," a putt of two feet or less that a friendly opponent declares does not have to be holed out.

GOBBLE: A putt that unexpectedly lands in the hole.

IN THE LEATHER: A putt closer to the hole than the distance between a putter's head and its grip. In friendly matches, an opponent may declare such a putt a gimmee.

MULLIGAN: A second shot off the tee, often permitted once in a casual round. Also known as a Shapiro.

POT BUNKER: A small, deep sand trap.

QUAIL HIGH: A long shot that has low trajectory.

RABBIT: A topped shot that bounces erratically. Also called a scooter.

RAINMAKER: A ball hit underneath that goes straight up into the air.

RUB OF THE GREEN: When a ball in motion is stopped or deflected by an outside agency. Another way of saying "tough luck."

SCLAFFING: Hitting the ground behind the ball, causing an embarrassing divot.

SCOOP: A bad swing in which the club head has a dipping or digging action.

SKULLING: Hitting a chip or pitch shot too hard and sending the ball past the green.

SKYWRITING: The act of making a loop or circle with the club head at the top of the backswing.

SNIPE: A sharply hooked ball that dives quickly.

STONY: A shot where the ball lands close to the flagstick.

STYMIE: In the past, this referred to the situation when one's putt was blocked by an opponent's ball. The rules have been changed so that the blocking ball can be lifted. Now the term refers to being blocked by a tree or other obstruction.

TAKING THE PIPE: Collapsing under pressure at the critical stage of a golf competition. Also called choking.

TIGER: Someone who is playing unusually well.

WHIFF: A complete miss of the ball on a swing. Also called a fan.

WHINS: A British term for heavy rough or brush.

YIPS: Convulsive shakes that cause the player to badly miss a putt.

The text of this book was set in
Scotch Roman by Beth Tondreau Design
of New York, NY.

Design by Beth Tondreau Design

Cover illustration by Gary Gianni
Illustrations hand-tinted by Gary Gianni